Countries

China

by Christine Juarez

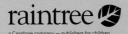

raintree
a Capstone company — publishers for children

Raintree is an imprint of Capstone Global Library Limited, a company incorporated in England and Wales having its registered office at 264 Banbury Road, Oxford, OX2 7DY – Registered company number: 6695582

www.raintree.co.uk
myorders@raintree.co.uk

Edited by Erika L. Shores
Designed by Bobbie Nuytten
Picture research by Wanda Winch
Production by Jennifer Walker

Printed in China
ISBN 978 1 4747 1977 3
20 19 18 17 16
10 9 8 7 6 5 4 3 2 1

British Library Cataloguing in Publication Data
A full catalogue record for this book is available from the British Library.

Photo Credits
Capstone, 4; Dreamstime: Hanhanpeggy, 15, Yunhao Zhang, 11; Shutterstock: AKaiser, cover, 1 (scalloped design), beboy, 17, fotohunter, cover, Hung Chung Chih, 9, JinYoung Lee, 19, Ohmega1982, back cover globe, Oleg_Mit, 22 (bill), ra3rn, 22 (coin), Teresa Kasprzycka, 13, Yu Lan, 22 (flag), Yuri Yavnik, 1, 21, zhu difeng, 5, 7

We would like to thank Gail Saunders-Smith, Ph.D., for her invaluable help in the preparation of this book.

Every effort has been made to contact copyright holders of material reproduced in this book. Any omissions will be rectified in subsequent printings if notice is given to the publisher.

All the internet addresses (URLs) given in this book were valid at the time of going to press. However, due to the dynamic nature of the internet, some addresses may have changed, or sites may have changed or ceased to exist since publication. While the author and publisher regret any inconvenience this may cause readers, no responsibility for any such changes can be accepted by either the author or the publisher.

Note to Parents and Teachers

The Countries series supports learning related to people, places and culture. This book describes and illustrates China. The images support early readers in understanding the text. The repetition of words and phrases helps early readers learn new words. This book also introduces early readers to subject-specific vocabulary, which is defined in the Glossary section. Early readers may need assistance to read some words and to use the Contents, Glossary, Read more, Websites and Index sections of the book.

Contents

Where is China?

China is the fourth-biggest country in the world. It's a little bit smaller than the United States.

China is in eastern Asia.

China's capital is Beijing.

Beijing ★

CHINA

Landforms and climate

China has rivers, mountains and deserts. Heavy rain helps plants grow along the Yangtze River. Snow falls in the Himalayas. Winds blow across the Gobi Desert.

Animals

Many rare animals live only in China. Giant pandas, golden snub-nosed monkeys, South China tigers and Chinese alligators are all at risk of dying out.

Language and population

China is home to more than 1.3 billion people. Most people in China speak Mandarin Chinese. This language has thousands of symbols.

Food

The Chinese enjoy fresh vegetables, fish and tea. They also eat soup, rice and noodles. People in China eat with chopsticks.

Celebrations

Chinese New Year is celebrated

in January or February. The celebration

lasts for 15 days. People watch

parades and fireworks. Some people

dress in dragon costumes.

15

Where people work

About half of China's people work as farmers. They grow rice, wheat and tea. Some people have jobs catching fish. In cities, most people work in factories.

Transportation

People ride bicycles in most cities in China. Buses and metro trains are busy too. People living in mountains might use horses to travel.

Famous sight

The Great Wall of China is thousands of kilometres long. It's the biggest thing ever built by people. People from all over the world visit the Great Wall every year.

Country facts

Name: People's Republic of China

Capital: Beijing

Population: 1,349,585,838 (July 2013 estimate)

Size: 9,596,960 square kilometres (3,705,407 square miles)

Language: Mandarin Chinese

Main crops: rice, wheat, potatoes, corn, peanuts

China's flag

Money: Yuan

Glossary

Asia largest of Earth's seven continents; a continent is a large landmass

capital city in a country where the government is based

Chinese New Year first day of the Chinese Lunar Calendar; a lunar calendar is based on the phases of the moon

chopsticks narrow sticks used to eat food; chopsticks are mainly used by people in Asian countries

factory place where a product, such as a car, is made

language words used in a particular country or by a particular group of people

metro system of underground trains in a city

symbol design or object that stands for something else

Read more

Mandarin (Languages of the World), Lucia Raatma (Raintree, 2012)

The Chinese Empire (Great Empires), Wayland Publishers (Wayland, 2015)

Websites

www.ancientchina.co.uk
Explore China's history on The British Museum's website.

ngkids.co.uk/places/30-cool-facts-about-china
Discover 30 fascinating facts about China.

Index